GW01605177

this

could

be

such

a

beautiful

world

Panda Prints.

ISBN 0 340 16547 2

First published in Great Britain 1972 by
Brockhampton Press Ltd, Salisbury Road, Leicester
First published in USA by Panda Prints Inc, New York

Printed by Fletcher & Son Ltd, Norwich
and bound by Richard Clay (The Chaucer Press) Ltd, Bungay

this could be such a beautiful world if . . .

the brooks

the streams

the rivers

the lakes

the very sea itself

were fresh

and clean

and sparkling

once again

the skies were clear

and blue by day

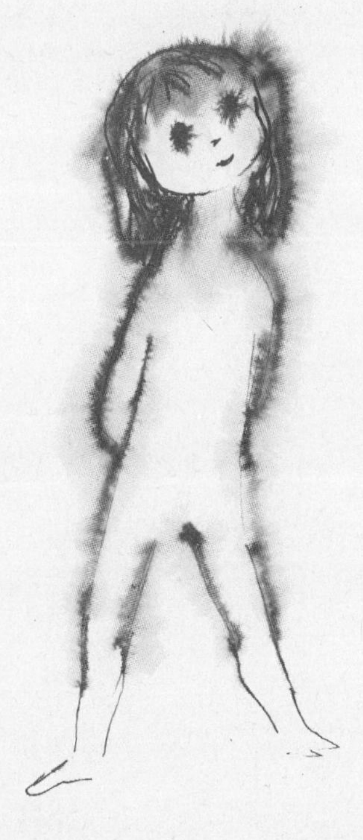

and filled with stars

at night

if the wind blew
sweet and pure
the rain was only
rain
the trees continued
to grow tall
on the hills
and the meadows
were knee deep
with daisies and clover

if the forests were alive

with animals

and the sky with birds

and the waters with fish

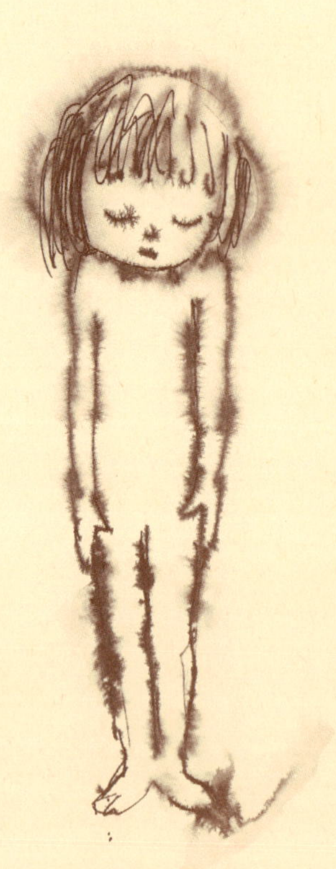

if people would only stop
hurting and hating
themselves
and those around them

if we could all care
just a little more
and fear just a little
less

if everyone could feel
just a little bit
for one another

of what I feel
towards You
and You feel
towards me

this could be such a beautiful world

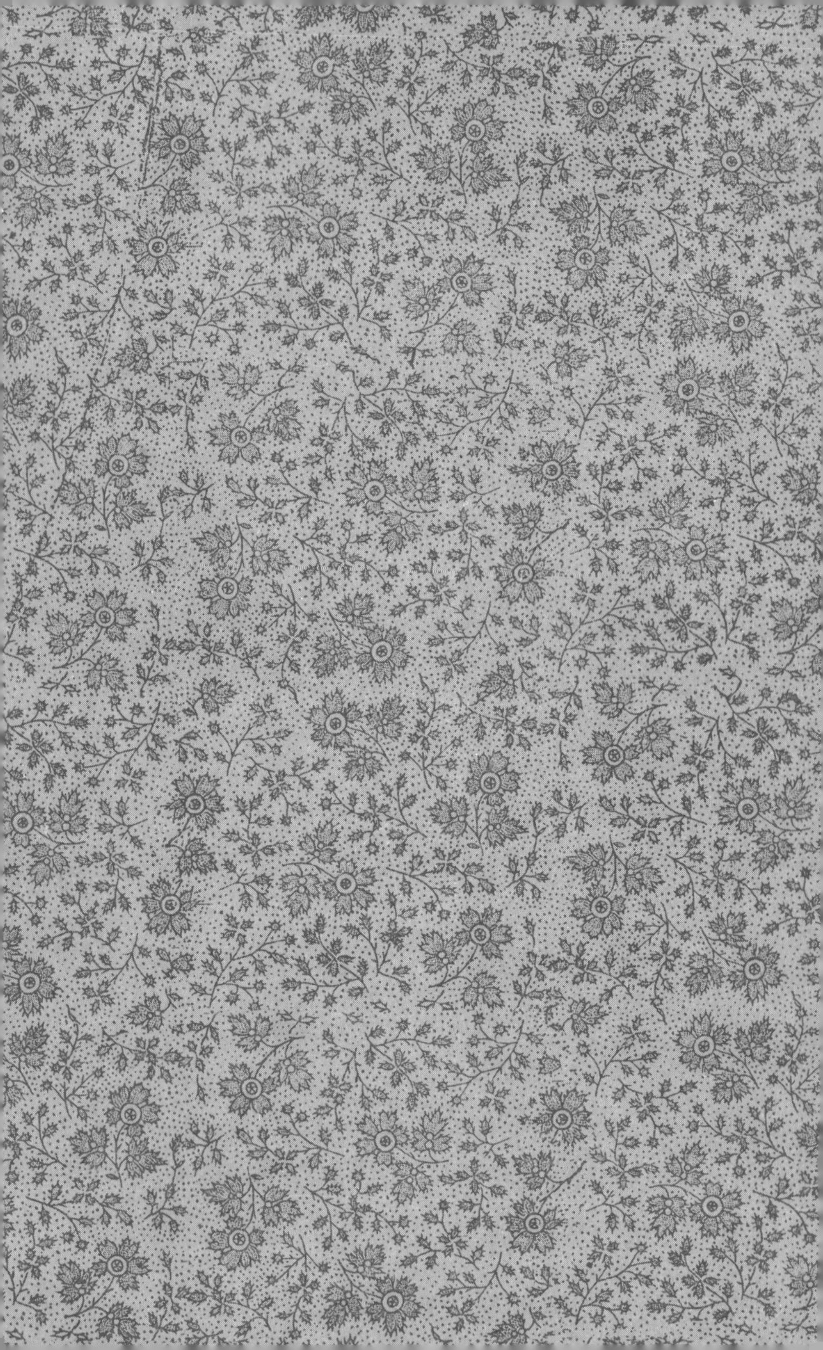